Not Yet Not

Anna Krushelnitskaya

Copyright © 2021 by Anna Krushelnitskaya
All Rights Reserved
ISBN: 978-1-64180-135-5
Cover art and design by Margaret Romano-Krushelnitskaya

Published by
Front Edge Publishing
42807 Ford Road, Canton, MI, 48187

DIARY DEARIE

This is the diary of my limbic system:
Took out your letters and photos and kissed them;
Took out your statues and started to dust them;
Nearly wrote you a note, as that is my custom;
Hated a little your lovers, the whole roster;
Took out the cutest lover and flossed her;
Put her back and cried, rockabilly hiccoughs;
Spared one evil thought to your random pickups;
Took out your current wife and nearly smacked her;
Didn't, although she definitely was a factor;
Remembered your words, shallow, unfair and low;
Cried a little, remembered I had some Merlot;
Remembered what day it was in my lunar rhythm;
Remembered my breathing exercises and breathed them;
Listened to *L.A. Woman,* noblesse oblige, and
This, my friend, is the story of cold fission.

THE LABELLUM

I saw the incidence of death, but not the increments of death, the tools and implements of death I knew were there, but did not ponder; just like the moon, it's always death, wanes, waxes, moons, it's always death, one analgesic day a month I do not see it, but it's yonder.

Some shut the curtain, but for me that veil is vanishing; I hope the lying dogs sleep at nightfall and don't wake death and all its proxies. We have to walk the balance beam 'tween being good and feeling good; I don't know if the curtain helps to walk this walk that really rocks us.

When I turned forty, my right eye began to do a weird thing, and then I saw I had been blind: from now to then, I have been dying. See the corpuscular brown crops, in Russia they are called buckwheat, upon my skin? These fleas, they spell that with the dogs I have been lying.

It'll take my toys away from me before it takes me from my toys, my eye will fail and further fail, my tires will pop, my brain will tire, all fun activity will cease, my hireability decrease, and Jezebel just one more job for which I never have been hired.

So I decided what to do: I will be pretty one last year. I'll wander in in furs, in tears, dreams, twinkles, nectar, touch of venom … Hide my unsightly overalls! I will perform twilightly strolls, a wet and orphaned orchid on a parched and wrinkled sea of denim.

I'll drink, pretending to deglaze the vessels death is trained to glaze, make tiny punctures in my skin, fill them with booze to depths Elysian, I'll buy fishnets and start to smoke, and then I will go up in smoke, the flying whore of Middle West, a dirigible of derision.

Beneath my helmet and panache, it's true, my irises are washed, one can see how my neck is knit, and time doth flit, and then it flyeth; so I will wipe my painted lip, and I won't give it any lip, and drift through birches white as sheets with Andrew, who's my favorite Wyeth.

RECOIL

Recoil!
How do you live with yourself?
You don't.
They do.
Do you sing "I Dreamt I Met a Galilean" in the shower?
(Guilty.)
Do you see the mole on your back?
(No.)
Do you say "uh" three times per sentence,
All day every day,
The en-ti-re
Sixteen years they've lived with you?
(Guilty.)
Sixteen years, and what do they get?
Do you sing "Sixteen Tons" in the shower?
(Guilty.)
Do you sing "Brown Eyed Girl" in the shower?
Do you see your long dark hair in the shower drain?
(Yes.)
All day, all year?
(Guilty.)
Do you cry in the shower?
Are you an unreasonable crier?
Do you sing "Cryin'" by Aero-frickin'-smith in the shower?
(As charged.)
Do you know how many times you told this story already?
You bake shitty things and throw them out.
You drive stupid.
You have age spots.
(Guilty.)

You think you are so smart.
Go.
Go.
Go do a silent retreat already.

A DRESS OF SUCCESS

There I stood in a dress, on a small dainty hill
I decided on love, so I stood in a dress
I decided on fame, so I stood on a hill
With my booty my beauty, my fortress, my buttress
My forte, my butter and bread
With my flowing tresses in glowing trusses
My trust fund, my treasure trousseau
In my gauzy chiffon, gazing hither and yon
Cutely clutching a clutch, a desirable lady
Hope someone took a picture, I looked like a winner
I looked like I could be a winner already
And the whole horizon was prettily dotted
Swiss-dotted with whispery wisps
With desirable ladies who were also running
Although they were standing on small dainty hills
And gossamer gossip power lines
Were webbing them into a web
And some were rotating with the façades always facing,
Façades always painted around and around
Men who looked very busy amid all this twisting and torsion
Men whose fascination lasts as long as the commercial
I stood there looking killer, looking like I have my crap together
Looking for someone to kiss me apart and then kiss me back together
And every once in a while a woman would start erupting in firsts:
First baptism, communion, prom, wedding dress
One pretty and the next one prettier, next one prettier still, has to be
Has to be or you lose, or you lose
And here and there were the old ones
With moth-eaten dresses on flea-bitten bodies on worm-ridden hills
And a woman would dismount the hill

And disappear
And I would look away
And clutch my sequined purse
And sequence my poses to the music
And twirl
(Or you lose, or you lose, or you lose)

MATERNITY WARD

I wore makeup in piles and scores
I punctuated checkered floors
Coloraturas of my scores
Could send a Boy Scout troop aflutter
I could have danced, have danced all night
A Broadway troupe fell left and right
Like dominos in black and white
A fan of cards to my staccato

My score of fans I'd idly browse
I'd rock Marika Roekk eyebrows
Ida Lupino lips and blouse
And Idared my apples cheeky
The seven changes—little black
Gabbana red, Gabbana black
Mañana red, Romana black
In heaven, cheek-to-sheik-to-chic-ey!

But it has washed me cleanly clean
Milk, Vaseline, milk, Listerine,
The tidal needs the tears marine
Blue eyes, white skin, nightgown and clean scent
Soft and transparent here I lie
On laundry lines I hang to dry
And in me you can't wrap a lie
But in me you can wrap an infant

DREAM DREAM TANGO

And one and two and three and four, who is this knocking on my door, the eyes are downcast, demure, the skirts are riding up, impure, your stocking seams, they laugh and tease, above your knees, below your knees, across the floor, across the floor, you're knocking harder on my door, stand still and nobody gets hurt, I run my hand across your shirt

Of velvet.

Extend!

He dips, she snaps, he dips, she snaps, she will need therapy, perhaps, your stocking seams, they burn and sear, my life revolves around you, dear, you are the gritty grain of sand 'round which this stunning pearl is built, the way you handle me, off-hand, the way off-kilter me you tilt, the way you flirt and then revert, I'm glad I ripped into your shirt

And found you.

Exalt!

A torn silk stocking on my knee, remember me, remember me, now break your gaze, avert your face, give me one very last embrace, his velvet touch, her lashing lace, one very-very last embrace, his victory—what is it for, her sadness dragged across the floor, now I have stopped, my heart is stopped, collect the pearls that I have dropped

And keep them.

Exhale.

AWAKE

When I'm asleep—when I'm asleep—the upper lid—the lower lid—when everything a point in time in space and goes into the tunnel

A needlepoint—a needle point—a needle eye —the camel through—the camel goes through pointy eye and goes right back into the tunnel

Then it unfurls—a leaf of tea—a tea of leaves—portending doom—a promise melody a threat and goes right back into the tunnel

I only dreamt of you three times and maybe never will again but when I dreamt of you three times you didn't make it to the picture

First dream—it was a worry dream, third dream—it was a gossip dream, they burrowed through my furrowed brain and then went back into the tunnel

The second was my favorite dream, it was a mute and lovely dream, you sent me something in a bag and something I could not decipher

And then I knew you were a gift, a gossip, worry, but a gift, and that is how I choose to see that something I cannot decipher

And then I close around the gift, I close my shell around the gift, and stash it in my furrowed brain and I go back into the tunnel

And every time the day is nuts, my weird one, then I take the shell and mutely look at what you chose to send me mutely—peacock feathers

SNOW WHITE

I'm ready
For anything
And if the only thing
You ever say to me is "darling"
I'll stay
Be happy when you're calling
Be nothing when there's nothing
In my mailbox
Your life important
Mine unused
Your life behind the fence
I run my stick against
To hear my days knocking off
A ring of sterling
Silver

I'm ready
For anything
And if the only thing
You ever say to me is "dinner"
I'll run with it
We'll do the usual
A ring of gold
Around the block—the fights, the square dance, the children
Will hate the sin, forgive the sinner
Everybody
Mows that lawn
They all
Have those dandelions

I'm ready
For anything
And if the only thing
You ever say to me is "never"
Well, then you are that kind of lover
I'll stay with it
All that is doable, the fever and the lava
Get thrown out that mouth
And then cool down, dry up, that sliver
That cinder
A fly in amber
A ring of sterling
Silver

FEDORA

Thank you Lord for this life and the shit that didn't come home to roost
The times I've made it to the bell, the teacher never found out
I've been a cocktail waitress with a sparkly bow on my ass
Forgive me Lord for I have sinned or not, whichever one
With my money my hands my pants my words my lips I have been loose
They sink ships I heard but I chancily wore my fedora like an umlaut
With a guise this size Lord I surmise I pass I pass I pass
I'm Death, I'm Explosion, I feel so big as if I'd swallowed the Sun

A HANDSOME COUPLE

In madras plaids and in seersuckers, a handsome couple, we'd be those fuckers, my lipstick careless, your eyebrow rogue, this month in Paris, next month in Vogue, cocktails and vomit, your laughter low, my every comment a sly bon mot, a game of bocce, five-o-clock shadow, our gamine urchins named Lark and Meadow, your highball turns eyeball whites to yellow, your stomach turns washboard hard to Jell-O, you slap me 'round in children's full view, I sleep around, I am in Bellevue, our rustic garden with urns of plaster, the kids are hiding, you slap me faster, the cash runs out and we crash the car and it's past checkout and it's sayonara

FIRST, YOU ARE A CHILD

You draw a whale.
It looks like a whale.
It looks like a whale, it looks like a whale, it looks like a whale, it looks like a whale.
It does not look like a whale.
You give up drawing.
You make pancakes.
You spit in the pan to see if the oil is hot enough, like your father showed you.
You spit in the pan.
You spit in the pan, you spit in the pan, you spit in the pan, you spit in the pan, you spit in the pan.
You do not spit in the pan.
You drizzle some water in the pan.
Someone calls you a bitch.
You fly off the handle.
You fly off the handle, you fly off the handle, you fly off the handle, you fly off the handle, you fly off the handle.
You don't fly off the handle.
You plough on, a patient Nurse Ratched.
You are afraid of drunk men.
You are afraid of drunk men, you are afraid of drunk men, you are afraid of drunk men, you are afraid of drunk men.
Never mind.

EXPRESSLY

You keep leaving me.
You keep leaving me everywhere.
You've left me on every park bench in town.
You can easily describe me:
I am red.
I am soft.
I am warm.
I have a hole in the top:
That's how the steam gets out.
Not very good at ownership, are you.
Often drunk and always careless.
Others have picked me out of the box,
Tried me on.
On a couple, I almost fit.

SEUSS

I broadcast something at midnight
It's hard to figure out
I am an outline filled with black
So black box beeps came out
I'll fix myself by this year's end
Whatever Sigmund said
I do not want to be a box
So I will be a blade

NOOSE

Away, where you can't hear the bombastic Fourth of July news,
Where the moon sweeps across the grass in a swath,
Can she sneak in with a hammer, a sickle, a noose
And take your peace, your wheat, your cattle, your cloth?
It's better that your life doesn't rhyme,
It's better that you entomb your sanity in cement,
It's better that you be of love indigent—
(I said don't rhyme!
Or does your love lie illiterate,
Invertebrate yet inveterate?
If you can hear the cadences, then
Shake your vials of Vicodin,
Small maracas!)
Where do you place the buoy?
Where do you capture the flag?
Is the worth of your life now?
Is the worth of your life later?
Is the worth of your life never?
Whatever.
Hi-five them in cubicles, in educated tenors:
Good game good game good game good game good game.
Turn off the lights in all of your five rooms:
Front room living room kitchen hallway bedroom.
She will explode in black licorice,
She will write yellow brick road.
The prairie is big enough for the both of you to part ways.
Sleep tight.

YOUR PRESENTS ARE NOT NEEDED

I would like to spend my life today
Have all proceeds go to picking up people's crap
Keeping the blinds dusted
Making sure no one gets upset
And towards guilt for when children get sick
Depressed unemployed
And a memorial plaque
Mom was this mom was that
You just couldn't say certain things to her
She had a quick temper
She went hypoglycemic on you
Mom did
She liked the table clean
I would like to spend my life today
Break it into smaller bills
Coins in a foreign currency
Smash it against the wall
You pick up the brittle bits
You say mom gave me these shards
These sharps
No you moron mom loved you
A woman you never knew gave you these
Leftover from her foreign life
Spent
Sent to you across the sea
Not in the same currency
Not in the same coin
Almost in the same amount
Save for some change she kept for herself
For dream pictures in her
Dark movie brain

WON'T COME OUT

I am supposed to be a shining pillar
A tall impeccable column of light
I've come up short I am short
I failed everyone
I ruined the show
Now my love will snap at the waist
Bending down to me to say how could you
Don't you see I'm breaking
Now my children will be dwarfs
And I will never reach God, and my
Short fingers will not touch His like the postcard
In the airport lounge showed they can
No new glittering tooth can rest on me
I fell short as a spoke
I fell short of breath as I spoke
Forgive me I'll leave
I'll just have a small drink and leave
Not the whole glass
Not a tall drink
A short one
And brown
Rye
I was supposed to be a pillar
A sequoia
But I am just rye
Like the whole field of us
Flattened
Smothered with rain

NOROVIRUS

Annie I wish you would stay around long enough for your name to become a habit of my mouth; Annie we're having a snowfall of marshmallow fluff, strange that it's come from the west and from the south; Annie sometimes you hollow me out to a husk, Annie open your window and throw me some bread; Annie Annie you are asleep at dusk, Annie that is a hazard for your head! Annie Annie you know it is not just you, Annie half of the town are now throwing up; Annie Annie you hollow me out I'm blue; Annie you must hydrate take a sip from this cup; Annie you never talk, you're as tight as a spy, that's why you never sleep and you are too thin; Annie open your mouth and let the cranes fly. Annie open your mouth and let my love in.

RECK

I'm feeling restless and reckless
Completely without any reck
To express this or keep this in check? What the heck
In the arches the wind it rustles
In the mountains the rain it rains
The hum in the muscles the drive in the veins
Let's go for a pint downtown
The stone it is growing moss
From here it's all down but I want it across
The consciousness she is beating
The consciousness she is a hive
The foliage is pretty let's go for a drive

WHAT FLAGS

What flags do you run up your stake?
What flags do you fly?
What news do you share?
The daily Lüscher,
But rarely the Swiss cross.
But often it's something that's crisscross,
Like scissors across a desire.
Sometimes a dead snake.
Sometimes a coat of arms, or just arms
Waving across the sky—come here!
An Inflatable Wacky Waving Tube Man.
Sometimes just a coat
Impaled on a steeple:
A scare-crow, a scare-people.
A weather-vane boat,
A weather-vane rooster, a weather-vane watering can.
Sometimes a sphere, the flag of Japan.
Sometimes just atmosphere.
Mama Bear Laura Ashley bloomers,
Diapers,
Socks,
Windsocks,
Sometimes a heraldic shield,
But mostly windshield wipers,
Broomers and groomers
Crisscross the sky
To keep me a clear
Field.

KILLED A CAT

A body's a body, and flesh is warm milk:
No secrets, a pleasure boat.
Lay down your arms and let down thy silk—
And that is all she wrote.
The mercury climbs from warm to high
And happily boils down to this:
Will my eye meet a curious eye
After we break the kiss?
Your body is fine, a pleasure mine,
A bath, a burrow, a nest—
But will your mind be dancing with mine
When my head falls asleep on your chest?
No treasure, no debt, my pleasure pet,
No problem, I'm glad, gesundheit.
But as we smoke-signal with cigarettes—
Will you turn-signal my light?
Can we speak directly? Can I be direct? Do I speak correctly? Do I be correct?
Your ashes are falling, your ashes are falling, your eyelids are falling, eyelashes I'm wrecked.
The Citgo outside is burning within and donuts are going stale.
I'll put my hand on your eyelids and spin.
I'll put my hand up for sale.

DRAWL

My broken engagement is broken.
I hurt like a peeled carrot.
I would hide at my Aunt's in Hoboken,
But cold and un-soothed, I can't bear it.
You wear your lips in a bow-tie,
I'll wear my skirt in a tulip.
You can take me out on a boat and I
Think I will take that mint julep.
The evening sun melts like a sundae.
I peel like a hurt carrot.
You tell me your uncle will run for DA.
My ring was a six-carat.
I am a befouled Hepburn.
I can tell up which tree you are barking.
Your drawl is a salve for my sunburn.
What the hell, you can take me parking.
You're a man of means and no virtue,
Of bourbon and a boutonniere,
My skirt will only just skirt you,
You're a fancier, a financier.
You don't know how hard it is for me.
I am finished, I'm ready to walk.
Take your hand off my knee and pour me
Another one on the rocks.

ALICE

When it's harder for one than it is for the other,
Hard to be the one for whom it is harder.
She has nothing to argue and nothing to barter.

She thinks she has written twice all the letters.
Sshhee tthhiinkkss sshhee has written twice all the letters.
She has done as her elders but not as her betters.

She has flirted with crazy, and crazy has flirted
Back, her brain not to code, all mis-wired and shorted,
Detained, medicated, and nearly deported.

She wipes down the bar, puts a shine on the chrome.
She locks up the diner and heads on home.
She can trust only knives made of Styrofoam.

MINUTES

There is a shortage of minutes, a shortage of mental means
You will look at the clock and not know what a clock means
You will want to write a note: please someone explain
But the letters will be obscure and the paper plain
You will look at the clock; it will look with a blank face
Arabic numbers gone down to null, to erase
You will look at the clock; it will clock you with blunt force
Roman numbers gone out in a Trojan horse
The white coat will say Agg-No-Zhah, but not to you
You will look at a pen and not know what to drive it through

COBALT

I am attentive
Aquamarine, ultramarine, I nearly splash, retain the rain, I am retentive
Of your moods
Oh of your blues, your baby blues, towards your sadness I'm attentive
To your waves
Your neuro waves, my neuro waves, the blue, the red, someone inclined could make a graph
I am inclined
Towards you ever so slightly, so my spare attentions could benevolently slide
Oh yes I see
You see, you mean it only slightly, only Tuesdays, not quite literally always—that's okay
I'm only watching
They are enlarged, attentive pupils, to make up for all the darkness and the fog
I'm only watching
You exit here, enter there, making tracks that shift from fox to rat to bear, you are wily
It is okay
I am attentive, it is only attention, see? The red, the blue, I'm only making
A graph
One day I'll stop you in your tracks and I will take your autograph and I will give you
A blue button

DELFT

I think by now I know more than I don't
The blows blew by that you so deftly dealt
A nebulous blue sun, a blue sailboat
Atop the lake in willows done in Delft

The shepherdess, the suitor, skirts of lace
Repeat the same forgetful blue gavotte
Repeat of tiles around the Dutch fireplace
Of our lakehouse that we have never bought

You want to be my conscience or my muse?
You wanted to be neither here nor there
Nor dexter, sinister, hypotenuse
Between the two; I do no longer care

The lake is still and blue, but life is fluid
The lake is still, like you, a picture only
I wish for it no more, so what, I blew it
I wish for it no more than I am lonely

MEN WHO BUILD FIREPLACES

You need us to be square pegs
Not fitting infinity holes.
You need us squares of square by square
We raise voices no higher than baritones.
When we hear of a torrid affair,
Our eyes of varied blue denim
See an imminent torrid nightmare
And we reach for the antivenom.
You are writing this poem drunk.
You are wearing drunk mascara.
You need us to build you a fireplace.
You need us as square as square.
We see your right face, left face, middle face.
You run short and fast, a greyhound.
Take a Baritone Minecraft Fireplace.
It will help you be quiet and round.

JEANS

Have you ever met anyone you had to leave?
For if you didn't leave then you would never leave?
You would follow this person all around universe
And nothing would ever get done?
You're just different enough: I got brains, you got looks,
And in general that type of interesting thing.
You would sit mesmerized, slipping, slipping to fall,
To fall into each other, and then there you'd be:
Two very tight people who wear cool jeans
And don't need anyone in the world?

So, you left that someone. You had to leave,
For if you didn't leave then you would never leave.
If you followed that person all around universe,
How would anything ever get done?
You're just different; one is a schemer, a crook,
And the other a blunderer-through, that's the thing.
It was very unwise, slipping, slipping to fall,
To fall into each other. So, then there you are:
Two very cool people in very tight jeans,
Who don't need anyone in the world.

MISERICORDE

We do not walk the Honest Path: you speak, and therefore you sneak. My Precious, you have caused my Wrath. My Precious, you should know I'm weak, and I will fight with Seven Words, and Wrath is just a Warning Sign, and I will smite with Seven Swords; the Dart of Wrath is brined in brine,

'twill swelter faster, fester, swell; Scammony Root to purge your Scams, but I know you, and know you well, you do not give two bleeding Damns about my Feelings, so you see, I'll give you sweet Complicity. My Thoughts and Feelings I won't flaunt, you will get only what you want.

Complicity's a fine Flambard, a sly Assault it does retard, it vibrates your vibrations back, against yourself your own Attack. Then, comes a Laugh Rapier so thin you do not feel it going in; you go about your business days and Nights, but word by word it weighs upon you; hurting, still you live, you Thief, a dripping bloody Sieve, and although Nettles is my Tongue, you cannot see where you were stung. Behind the Veil, behind the Fence, behind the Babalon Incense (you called me Whore; my heart is black)— Dogbane for Love and Heart Attack.Seduction's Javelin obeys: its tip comes off and then it stays. Your games are such low-level games—you are my Game; you're now in Flames. To help me through these Murky Waves—Cutlass of Grace; oh, Grace enslaves! To help me catch you, Slippery Fish—Trident of Kindness; oh, you'll wish,

after I'm done with all the Love, that you would kiss my Fencing Glove, but Silence is my Seventh Sword—it isn't a Misericorde! You walk yet cannot walk away; you're not allowed to stay yet stay; there is a Wound but no Offense; don't care what happens to you hence.

LIARS

Liars don't have plans long form.
Liars live hour to hour.
They hotfoot from platform to platform
Between trains about to go south or sour.
Gotta paper the chinks in the splintering nest:
"Funny that you should ask about it, honey!"
Gotta duck out of that one, whistle over the rest
And lie lie lie lie fast like a bunny.

LUNCH BREAK

Lover why do you smolder on me
Lover why do you hold on for me
Five more minutes of our break, don't leave, you wound not
Lover I don't want to be a swine
Do me a favor, I don't want to be a swine
Lover-swan won't favor me the swine, she would not

Lover oh what a desk you have
Do you even understand what desk you have
Its varnished beaches are pulling down my tors-o
Lover if I were to nestle my nose into your neck
Lover it would all slide under the desk down to heck
In the same direction as the nap of your furs

In the shop I will whisper old curiosities
Calculate differences and die of jealousies
In your neck I will whisper silly piquancies
Ornament your ears with Oriental perjuries

We have five seconds left, and we don't need your calculator
A pencil has five second rings
And we don't need a radiographer
My one ring's already below the equator
Five seconds of your life, my-swan-my-soul
I will be your most breathless biographer

GUESS WHAT

I'm not very good at sharing but I'm good at giving away
It's impossible to offend me but it's easy to piss me off
My greatest surprise was the longer I lived the sadder I would become
And also the world got stupider and louder than I could take

To only reach for something, ask for someone when things are shitty—it is unfair
But just 'cause you're not a believer does not mean you can't understand or make a prayer
And I am heartbroken, I only want to lie with my back in the steady lap of you, close my eyes and not know the first thing
Because if I turn my face up around you never look believably true, and I always know you're a lost thing

DIAGNOSTIC/STATISTICAL

Because I feel that way the world is made of danger the world is made of treacle the world is baked of clay

Because I feel that way I feel things like a radar I feel that what I feel is true because I feel that way

Because I am perceptive I feel that I'm perceptive and since I'm so perceptive my feelings never fail

The dummies and the liars and the energy vampires the sheep and the deniers have been opening my mail

SMALL FRY

You remember them flailing around each other like two amoebas of judgement and praise judgement praise judgement fear judgement fear fear of judgement desire of praise distrust of praise preventative judgement slap retraction in fear of a retributive judgement slap

You remember them pushing on the air around your shoulders head and neck

You remember them pulling on your legs stretching you flat like you're gum

You remember them slapping wet j'accuse floor rags at your feet

You remember your breaths only going half-in

You remember your stomach ulcerating

You remember sitting tied up

By the shuffles

In the kitchen

On the bed

Retracting

Your skin

Shrink

Wait

Till

You

Are

Big

And

Out

'RITHMETIC

If you and I have a difference, and to find what it is you have to subtract me, then in order to remain positive you will have to assume that I'm less than you.

If you assume that we are not equal, then in order to remain positive you will have to assume that I am less than you.

If you have to subtract me, you cannot assume we are equal, because then you'll be left a zero.

If you choose to subtract yourself, instead, and we are both positive where I am bigger than you are, then you will leave me smaller, which is not a noble deed by most standards.

If you choose to subtract yourself and we are both positive where I am smaller than you are, then we will end up in a negative situation, for sure.

If you choose to subtract yourself and somehow make a positive difference, you have to assume that you are negative, and that's beyond most.

If you assume that we are both negative, you want to subtract yourself, and make a positive difference, then you have to assume I am more negative than you are.

The best subtraction operation for you is to declare yourself positive, me negative, and subtract me.

BONNIE CREATURES

All the pretty cupcakes
All the bonnie creatures
First, you get the outtakes
Late, you get bonus features
Apple blossoms cigarette butts
Paper pigeon stool
Idly float upon your vast
Reservoirs of cool
Pilot sketches, half-close dances
Eyebrows wiggle and furrow
Projected romances
Aborted on the morrow
Tentative smiles small puffy lint
Strokes not full but mini
This one'd be good in an apocalypse
This, for a week in Santorini
Wine and cakes for gentlemen
Hay and corn for huddled masses
A cup of ale for good old wives
Two cups of ale for good old wives
Three cups of ale for good old wives
And kisses—for the lasses

CANARY ISLES

Our birdie named Birb died; he couldn't spell his own name
The house is full of sobbing children
The cage curtains are drawn, the orange hearse
Yes lovey, but from now on everything will be like you always imagined it
Yes lovey, it will be five hundred million years before we die
Yes I will live in an orangery, a conservatory, redolent with citrus and blooming with parakeets parrots canaries, my own canary isles
Yes you will come and have orange-blossom tea with me from gold-rimmed bone china teacups
I will be spry white wise
You will never need to take care of me
I will never piss myself, never forget words letters numbers, any of your golden hairs, all of them in silver lockets
I will never forget you
We will never be those people who live together as baby monkey and monkey mama
And then never see each other again because they don't like each other's thoughts
It's just what happened today, it was highly irregular
Yes lovey, in my old age of ivory, a canary conservatory, a whole rookery, a sanctuary of birds under triangles of glass and refracted light
A goldmine of canaries

CODE

I have my own code; I keep it secure
Within its intact hide
You stood within reach on the edge of the shore
With a tiny me in your eye

You waved at me across the wooded gap
A new wind blew through the brush
My heart crumpled up like a paper scrap
And threw itself out in the trash

I stood untouched; the river's sheath
Didn't wrinkle under the snowfall
Like a Wolf-Rayet eye, you walked through the trees
Getting farther but not getting small

A fracture, the end, cellulose and lead
From my heart to the humus and water
Support me, trees, it's here where I freeze
With my unbroken code in order

CODE II

Why did you hide and make me go?
Did you revoke it?
I know I punched in the right code.
And you re-locked it.
I saw the light; the curtain moved,
And something flitted.
And everybody lies to me.
And I am liquid.
I didn't plan to wreck your life
Or cut your hair.
I only wanted to see you
Sit in your chair.
I waved across the wooded gap;
Hard wind was blowing.
I only thought then that you were
Someone worth knowing.
Yes, it is true I'm old and sad,
But why the padlock.
I do take care of myself.
I'm my own pet rock.
Maybe you poorly understand
Self-preservation.
Maybe you don't know you've shut out
A desperation.
No see, no hear, no touch from me;
Dog-whistle, maybe.
When we hang up, it is still me,
Your roiling baby.

CODE III

Your hand is curved up 'round an egg-shaped void
Should I reach and warm the egg with my hand?
What bird are we hatching?
A red-lettered round robin? They say language is code
The red-headed had a league, while the dancing men
They had an adventure.
I can keep my violin, my pipe, my orange pips
But what was it for, then?
What did I say: was it fine font, or was it small print?
Forgive me I'm foreign.
It's not that I don't understand complicated treatise
But I will be always aware of the pull of the floor, and
If we build that tower, I want to know
What it is for, or for what it is.
Forgive me I'm foreign.

PENTIMENTI

You are so well-written
With lovely errata
Pockmarks
Pentimenti
You are so well-written
Not fallen
In Eden
A little bit fading
You are so well-written
A manual
Teaching
To lose the un-earned
So well-written
You're sparkling
With Stendhal's crystals
In salty snow
The snowplow circling
The crows
You're soon ending

WHERE HER TOWEL IS

You said, do you love me or not.

I said, define love.

You said, do you love me or not.

I said, you don't understand. I have too many words on the subject. I'm afraid you wouldn't care, and you might get pissed off.

You said, but do you love me or not.

I said, sh-sh-sh. Can't you see? I don't know where my towel is.

You said, it should not be this hard to know.

I said, the love animals want to pet each other, and if we could take them out of us and set them on the table over there, the sex would pretty much continue to have itself. But our persons, empty of the naked and slippery love animals, would hate each other.

You said, so you don't love me.

I said, birdie, please. I'm here, aren't I.

You said, so you don't like me as a person.

I said, and this is precisely why.

You said, well that's lovely to know.

I said, I told you I had many words on the subject, you wouldn't care, and you would get pissed off. You scan what I say for mentions of your name and discard the rest. I could be reciting the Magna Carta and you would have no idea what I was saying because your name doesn't pop up. I always know when you stop tracking the conversation. Your face changes.

I said, oh God what did I just say. I'm sorry I'm sorry I'm sorry.

You said, wow. Wow.

I said, but if the love animals within don't want to pet each other, then you can sit your empty and perfectly sympathetic person bags together on the couch, and they can watch TV. They won't pet each other. But they won't beat each other up either. While the two love animals lower their body temperatures and go into anabiosis.

You said, you drive me up the wall.

I said, I told you I don't have just one word.

LADYFINGERS

Like a trifle, it was all built up from sponge.
And I miss those days when I used to beat the streets.
And I miss the yellow leaves padding the black.
And I miss peeking over your fence to see if you're there.
And I miss peeking through the glass to see the stuff
Of your apartment, what blankets, or chairs, or cats.
And I miss dropping six warm quarters into the slot,
And getting the fat Sunday paper in its yellow sleeve.
I miss all the bathrooms smelling like gingerbread,
And the dryer chutes shooting vanilla into the streets,
And reading the circulars for back-to-school sales,
And stacking the Tetris of cereals over the stove.
I miss the time before it all went rolling down
And up, and to pot, and bloomed a herpetic rose,
And they closed Borders the book store, and tumors grew,
And my hands can't hold this many things, as it turns out,
Ladyfingers in custard all thumbs, and things went slip.
And I miss having half my skull empty, in which to read,
And I miss walking to the drugstore with snow and dusk.
And I hope we can speak for a sec of how sad we are.
I miss having nothing but quarters, a book, and a cold,
The time after I was young and before I was old.

HAPPY NEW YEAR

One more hour, one more day, one more month, one more year
Disappear in the distance
One more friend, one more love, one more pet, one more child
One step closer to gone from existence
Would you terribly mind and allow one more time
To hold your face sweetly
Make a memory print of your eyes before time
Erases your features completely?
The clock strikes twelve, then the clock strikes two:
An illusion of a reversal
But look at yourself, you have wrinkled into
A decidedly beautiful person!
Here is one from the time you were terrified,
Here is one from the time you were sad
Those were funny times but I don't know if I'd
Do it over again, like I said
Here is one from the time you abandoned all hope
From the time your cried yourself blind
If we do have to tumble down this slope
Hold my hand like I like Iike I like like I like like I like it
Intertwined
Let us lie in deep silence and drunkenly stare
At Christmas lights twinkly and winky
While time goes running away down the stairs
Flipping over itself like a slinky
Yes I know you've been bad—what an odyssey is
This Las Vegas of fear and loathing
Do not cover yourself because modesty is
Only vanity in sheep's clothing
The clock strikes twelve, then the clock strikes two,

The Yule Log is spitting and hissing
I am flawed you are flawed I invite you to
Skip the pageant and get down to kissing
Cause sometimes you wanna be glorified
Other times you just wanna be held
Those were funny times, but I don't know if I'd
Do it over again, like I spelled
Here is one for the time you abandoned all hope
For the time your cried yourself blind
If we do have to tumble down this slope
Hold my hand like I like Iike I like like I like like I like it
Intertwined

www.ingramcontent.com/pod-product-compliance
Lightning Source LLC
Chambersburg PA
CBHW022122090426
42743CB00008B/963